W9-CDX-530

Secret Life of Rats

Rise of the Rodents

Trevor Day

Capstone press

Mankato, Minnesota

Fact Finders is published by Capstone Press,
a Capstone Publishers company.
151 Good Counsel Drive, P.O. Box 669,
Mankato, Minnesota 56002.
www.capstonepress.com

First published 2008
Copyright © 2008 A & C Black Publishers Limited

Produced for A & C Black by
MONKEY PUZZLE MEDIA Ltd   Monkey Puzzle Media Ltd
The Rectory, Eyke, Woodbridge
Suffolk IP12 2QW, UK

Library of Congress Cataloging-in-Publication Data

Day, Trevor.
  The secret life of rats : rise of the rodents / by Trevor
Day.
    p. cm. -- (Extreme science)
  Includes bibliographical references and index.
  Summary: "Discusses rats' features, their behavior and
lifestyle, their historical interaction with humans, and
their place in modern culture"--Provided by publisher.
  ISBN-13: 978-1-4296-3126-6 (hardcover)
  ISBN-10: 1-4296-3126-0 (hardcover)
  ISBN-13: 978-1-4296-3146-4 (softcover pbk)
  ISBN-10: 1-4296-3146-5 (softcover pbk)
1. Rats--Juvenile literature. I. Title. II. Series.

QL737.R666D39 2009
599.35--dc22

2008024364

Editor: Steve Parker
Design: Mayer Media Ltd
Picture research: Laura Barwick
Series consultant: Jane Turner

This book is produced using paper that is made from
wood grown in managed, sustainable forests. It is natural,
renewable, and recyclable. The logging and manufacturing
processes conform to the environmental regulations of
the country of origin.

Printed in the United States of America

The author wishes to acknowledge the assistance
of the National Pest Technicians Association, UK

Picture acknowledgements
Alamy pp. 1 (Picture Partners), 11 (David Kilpatrick), 15
(Alan King/2d), 17 (Steve Davey Photography), 18 (Pep
Roig), 22 (Picture Partners), 28 (Andrew Butterton);
Corbis pp. 7 (Terry Whittaker), 14 (Hulton-Deutsch
Collection), 27 (Swim Ink 2/LLC); FLPA p. 25 (S., D., &
K. Maslowski); Getty Images pp. 4 (Jeff Mermelstein), 12
(Time and Life Pictures), 24 bottom (S. Lowry/University
of Ulster), 29 top (Peter Lilja); Nature Picture Library
pp. 5 (Andy Sands), 6 (Dave Bevan), 8 (David Kjaer), 10
(Reinhard/ARCO), 19 (Toby Sinclair), 20 (Warwick
Sloss), 23 (Steimer/ARCO), 29 bottom (Dave Bevan); PA
Photos p. 24 top (Bebeto Matthews/AP); Photographers
Direct p. 9 (Cynthia Sauvageot); Rex Features p. 16
(24/7 Media); Science Photo Library p. 13 (Dr. Tony
Brain); Still Pictures pp. 5 inset (Daniel Heuclin/Biosphoto),
21 (G. Delpho/Wildlife IFE), 26 (Paul Glendell).

The front cover shows a brown rat in a sewer pipe
(NHPA/Stephen Dalton).

Every effort has been made to contact copyright holders
of material reproduced in this book. Any omissions will be
rectified in subsequent printings if notice is given to the
publishers.

CONTENTS

Abbreviations   **m** stands for meters   •   **ft** stands for feet   •   **cm** stands for centimeters
in stands for inches

Waste not; want not

One person's trash is a feast for a rat, or two or three rats . . .

Rats have lived alongside people for thousands of years. They, like us, eat a mixture of meat and vegetables. So people's waste scraps make great rat food. A hungry 10-ounce (283-gram) rat can eat one-third of its body weight in 24 hours. What it doesn't eat now, it stores in a food chamber in its burrow home.

In many rich countries, each person throws away up to half a ton of garbage per year. About one-fifth is food and garden waste, and one-third is paper and cardboard. Added together, this means more than one-half of household garbage is rat food!

What is a rat?

A rat is a type of **rodent**, which is a **mammal** with gnawing teeth.

rodent mammal with upper and lower front teeth that grow continually for gnawing

Smell is the rat's most powerful sense.

Large eyes can see in the dark.

Big ears pick up faint sounds.

Front teeth are long and sharp for gnawing.

Sensitive whiskers feel in the dark.

A rat's teeth are so strong that they can gnaw through some metals.

mammal backboned animal with hair; mothers feed their young milk.

5

Rats everywhere (almost)

Love 'em or hate 'em, you're probably never far from a rat.

Rats have reached nearly all the world's continents. They follow the spread of people, who accidentally provide rats with the food and shelter they need. "Facts" about rats are often made up. For example, there is not a rat for every person in the world. New York City, which has about eight million people, contains about one quarter of a million rats. Even so, just one rat can do a lot of damage.

Fast breeder

Under ideal conditions, with plentiful food and no predators to eat them, a pair of rats can leave behind more than one thousand descendants in a year.

Rats bite through electric wires, causing fires and power failures. They also nibble food stored in kitchens and cause health hazards.

predator creature that hunts other creatures for food

Rats can breed when only nine weeks old.

In one year, a female rat can produce up to 12 **litters**, each with 6–14 young.

A mother or father rat attacks almost anything that disturbs the nest.

Rat pups are hairless, blind, and deaf at birth.

As they grow, the young can fend for themselves within a month.

descendant living thing related to one that lived in the past

Led by the nose

If you're a rat, you spend much of your life with your nose close to the ground.

Step into the rat's world for a moment. If you're an adult rat, you are interested in food, a place to sleep, plus a mate, family, and friends. Your eyesight isn't great, so things more than a couple of feet away are blurry. You rely mostly on smell, hearing, touch, and taste, because much of the time you're running around in the dark, and your burrows and nests are gloomy.

Rats are careful about eating anything unfamiliar. A rat can't vomit. When tasting something unusual, it takes a nibble and waits. If it gets ill, it might eat soil to soak up the harmful food. It won't touch that food again.

Yum!

Yum! Yum!

urine liquid waste produced by an animal

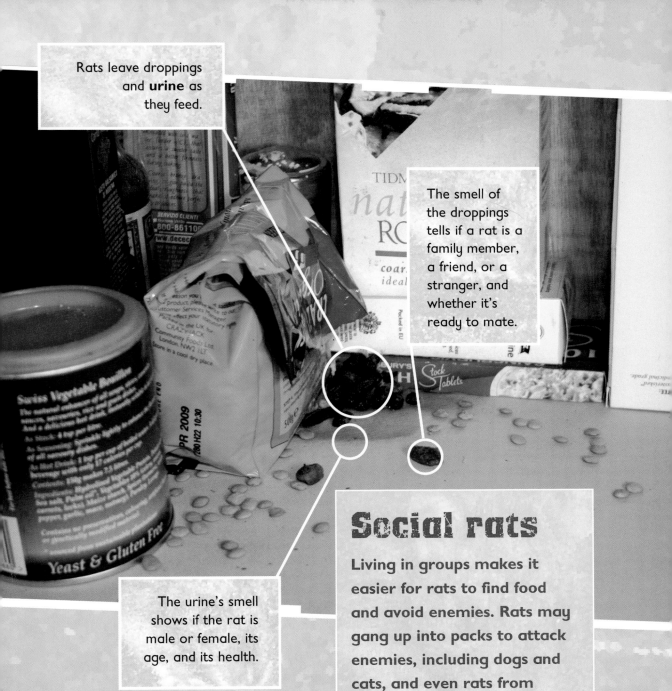

Rats leave droppings and **urine** as they feed.

The smell of the droppings tells if a rat is a family member, a friend, or a stranger, and whether it's ready to mate.

The urine's smell shows if the rat is male or female, its age, and its health.

Social rats

Living in groups makes it easier for rats to find food and avoid enemies. Rats may gang up into packs to attack enemies, including dogs and cats, and even rats from another pack.

All aboard!

If rats on a ship start to panic, there's something to worry about. They think their home is about to be flooded. Rats really do leave a sinking ship!

In the days of sailing ships, holes and hideaways below deck were great places for rats to live. They came out at night and nibbled any food scraps lying around. They gobbled up cockroaches and other insects. To stave off hunger, they gnawed rope or wood.

The brown rat (Rattus norvegicus) shown above is the most common rat today. It originally came from China and has spread worldwide. The black or ship rat (Rattus rattus) is the second most common. It's smaller than the brown rat with a narrower snout and longer tail. Originally from India, it was common in medieval Europe.

Why "ship rat?"

On ships, the black rat is a better survivor than the brown rat. It's smaller, climbs well, and needs less food and water, which are both in short supply on long voyages.

A black rat out in daylight is unusual. Rats are usually more active in the dark.

A rat scampers up a ship's rope.

Sharp claws grip well.

A long tail helps to balance and hold on.

Black Death

Between 1347 and 1351, about one-third of European people died from a disease spread by rats—the Black Death.

In 14th-century Europe, streets were strewn with rotting food. People often used a bowl for a toilet and then simply tipped the mess out of the nearest window. Black rats thrived in the stench and litter. They had fleas that carried **microbes** that caused the bubonic **plague**. The rats didn't suffer much from this illness. But when the fleas bit humans, they gave the people the deadly disease.

Bubonic plague caused coughing, fever, exhaustion, and swelling in the neck, armpits, and groin. So many people died that they were tipped into big holes called plague pits, burned, and buried.

A deathly name

The name Black Death shows how dreadful the disease was. Patches of skin turned dark because of bruising and rotting.

microbe microorganism; tiny living thing that one needs a microscope to see

12

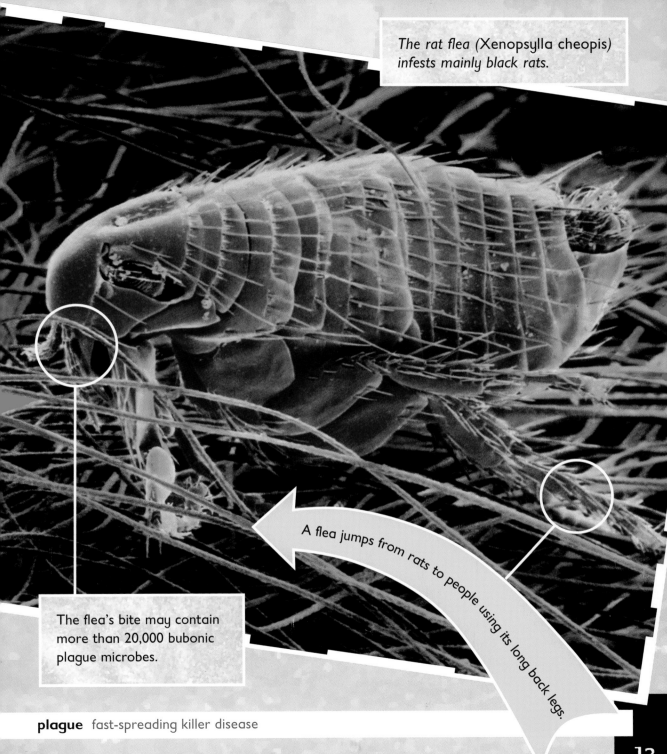

The rat flea (Xenopsylla cheopis) infests mainly black rats.

The flea's bite may contain more than 20,000 bubonic plague microbes.

A flea jumps from rats to people using its long back legs.

plague fast-spreading killer disease

Victorian rats

In Victorian times, rats were big money. Rat-catchers got paid for removing unwanted rats.

In 19th-century England, being a rat-catcher was an unpleasant job, looked down on by many people. But there were rich pickings. Pub owners wanted wild rats for their rat-baiting dens, while society ladies wanted specially bred black-and-white rats as pets.

*Through the ages, rat-catchers flushed rats out of holes and burrows using trained **ferrets**. Nets over the burrow entrance caught rats trying to escape.*

The yellows

If rat-catchers were bitten, rat urine could enter the wound. When this happened, the rat-catchers sometimes died of "the yellows," a disease caused by **bacteria** spread by rats. It damaged the liver, causing the skin to turn yellow. Today, this disease is called Weil's disease, or leptospirosis.

ferret weasel-like animal

Rat-catching was a difficult, smelly, and sometimes dangerous job, but often paid well.

Ferrets are slim enough to follow rats into their burrows.

Rats were caught by terriers and other dogs.

Cages caught the rats alive for rat-baiting, with bets on how many rats a dog could kill.

bacteria common small microbes, some of which cause disease

Sprung traps killed the rats.

Rat-a-touille

Ratatouille is tasty, but it doesn't really contain rats! It's a French vegetable dish with onions, tomatoes, peppers, and eggplant. However, some people really DO eat rats ...

In most countries, people only eat rat if they are starving and desperate. However, of the 56 types or **species** of rat, many are eaten by somebody, somewhere. In Ghana, West Africa, people hunt and also breed cane rats, which provide about half of the local meat supplies. People commonly eat rats in parts of India and East Asia, on some South Pacific islands, and in South Queensland, Australia.

This young rat ended up in a pickle—a jar of pickles. It goes to show that rats can get almost anywhere, and in this case, curiosity killed the rat!

Rat on the menu

Rats that live in French wine cellars are sometimes killed and soaked in wine before being grilled. In parts of northern Europe and Russia, the stew called "rats in cream" is a local favorite.

species living things that look similar and breed to produce offspring that themselves can breed

Mmm! Rat!

The rat's insides are removed, and it is roasted or perhaps grilled.

One or two large rats are enough for a meal.

Rat flesh tastes like a cross between pork and chicken.

17

Temple rats

To some people, rats are sacred, and they are treated like royalty.

In Deshnok, India, there is a **Hindu** temple dedicated to the rat goddess, Karni Mata. Inside the temple are 20,000 rats, cared for by priests. Hindu people from all over the world come to visit. They must take off their shoes before entering. If a temple rat scampers over your foot, that's a sign of good fortune. Spotting one of the temple's rare white rats is even luckier.

Miracle rats?

In the hundred or so years since Deshnok Temple began, there has been no outbreak of human disease spread by its rats.

If you step on or kill a temple rat by accident, you are expected to buy a model rat of silver or gold, or give an offering. This makes up for your wrongdoing.

Hinduism traditional Indian religion in which supreme beings take many forms, including animals

The temple rats are mostly tame and gentle.

Priests put out food and drink for the rats each day.

Sewer rats

In some places, there are very good reasons to check the toilet before you go ...

Rats that live in sewers are among the most dangerous. Spending so much time in and around human waste, they carry human diseases on their feet and fur, and in their urine.

Sewers are underground channels that carry away wastes from our toilets, sinks, and drains. In some places, they are more than 150 years old. As the sewer's brickwork crumbles, rats can climb up the pipes or drains into people's homes to look for food scraps. Some people go into the bathroom or cellar to find large rats scampering around!

Go anywhere

Rats are almost unstoppable. They can climb up pipes, squeeze through holes 1.5 inches (4 centimeters) across, and swim for hours on end.

sewer underground channel that carries human waste to the treatment plant

The tail works like a tightrope walker's pole, helping the rat to **balance.**

A rat uses its claws, flexible body, and tail to twist and turn as it climbs.

Rats can fall 50 ft (15 m) and land without harm.

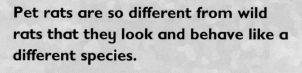

Pet rats

Pet rats are so different from wild rats that they look and behave like a different species.

Pet rats are descended from wild brown rats. But they come in lots of colors, and they are smaller, cleaner, and friendlier than wild rats. They are also clever, easy to keep, and have individual personalities. And they laugh . . . sort of. When playing with each other, or when tickled by their owner, rats make high-pitched chirping sounds that we can't hear. Scientists say this behavior is controlled by parts of the rat's brain that, in humans, are linked to laughter.

Pet rats become very friendly with their owners!

Lab rats and space rats

After mice, rats are the second most common laboratory animals used in experiments. They were also used on space missions, and many died in space. In 1969, people's complaints put an end to this practice.

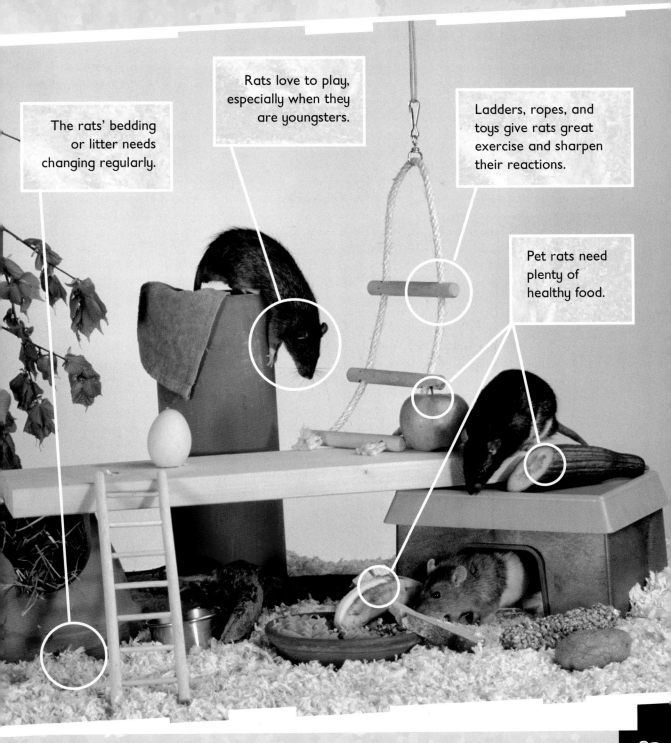

The rats' bedding or litter needs changing regularly.

Rats love to play, especially when they are youngsters.

Ladders, ropes, and toys give rats great exercise and sharpen their reactions.

Pet rats need plenty of healthy food.

Rats in restaurants

Rats in restaurants are unhealthy. In February 2007, a dozen rats ran riot in a fast-food restaurant in New York City—and became TV stars!

Attracted by food, rats enter restaurants under cover of darkness. Health inspectors visit regularly and look for signs such as gnawing, scratch marks, soiled food, urine, and droppings. In Greenwich Village, inspectors discovered that rats had got into the restaurant through holes when it was closed. They were well fed from waste food stored in bags, which the rats could easily gnaw through.

TV cameras captured the action in New York City as rats scampered around chairs and tables in this restaurant.

Diseases spread by rats include salmonella and listeria, which are types of food poisoning. They are caused by rod-shaped bacterial microbes like these.

Wild rat urine and droppings get mixed up with the foods that rats eat.

Rat urine and droppings can be packed full of disease-causing microbes.

People can pick up disease microbes on their fingers as they handle the food.

Rat feet trample disease-ridden urine wherever they run.

Rats eat or spoil food at any stage, from the growing crop, to transported or stored produce, to food after it's been cooked.

Rabid rats

Rats have been known to carry the killer disease rabies. If a wild rat bites you, quickly see a doctor.

To trap a rat

In 1936 the head of the American rat-catchers' organization changed the name of their job from "exterminator" to "pest controller." Why?

CLANG! Trap slams shut.

Rat cannot gnaw through the steel cage and escape.

Food bait tempts rat into trap.

immune able to fight off the harmful effects of a poison or disease

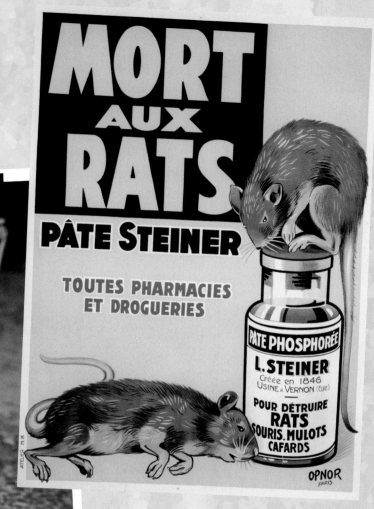

"Death to Rats!" Poisoned bait might kill rats, but it can be dangerous. Children and other animals might touch or swallow it.
*In any case, some rats learn to avoid the bait, while others are resistant or **immune** to the poison.*

The chief rat-catcher knew you couldn't kill all rats. You could only control their numbers. The best way is to stop giving them food. As long as there are scraps that rats can reach, and somewhere to hide and breed, they will flourish. Rats can be killed with poison. Or they can be trapped and then released far away. But rats are intelligent and learn to avoid poison and traps. You'll never catch them all.

The cost of rats

New York City spends more than $12 million a year controlling rat numbers. That's more than $1.50 for each New Yorker. In return, the city rats bite more than 150 people each year.

Keep rats in their place

Wild, pet, or lab, rats are here to stay . . . How do we keep rats at bay? There are a few things you can do to stop them from moving into your house.

Sort household waste by type.

Hungry rats eat almost anything, even orange peels and paper towels.

Store waste that rats might eat in pest-proof containers.

Food left out for hedgehogs and other wild animals can attract rats, so bring it in as darkness falls.

Rat farm

Some experts say that one-fifth of all food produced by farmers is eaten or spoiled by rats. The total loss adds up to billions each year.

The best way to deal with wild rats is to avoid attracting them in the first place. Stockpiles of wood or other garden waste make great rat homes. Don't leave out pet food or other food overnight. Make sure food is stored securely, and there are no small openings where rats could enter. More than half of domestic waste is leftover food, garden cuttings, paper and cardboard, which are all food for rats. Recycle or dispose of it properly. Keep rats at bay!

How do you do?

A rat can squeeze through openings much smaller than this—any gap it can fit its head through.

Glossary

bacteria common small microbes, some of which cause disease

descendant living thing related to one that lived in the past

ferret weasel-like animal

Hinduism traditional Indian religion in which supreme beings take many forms, including animals

immune able to fight off the harmful effects of a poison or disease

litter a group of animal babies born at the same time

mammal backboned animal with hair; mothers feed their young milk

microbe microorganism; tiny living thing that one needs a microscope to see

plague fast-spreading killer disease

predator creature that hunts other creatures for food

rodent mammal with upper and lower front teeth that grow continually for gnawing

sewer underground channel that carries human waste to the treatment plant

species living things that look similar and breed to produce offspring that themselves can breed

urine liquid waste produced by an animal

KEEP RATS AT BAY!

1. Waste items that attract rats include almost any fresh or thrown-away food (meat or vegetables), garden or kitchen waste, and paper and cardboard.

2. Prepare just enough food for people to eat, so that there is little or no waste. (This saves money too!) Carefully dispose of any cooked waste.

3. Put uncooked scraps, such as fruit and vegetable peelings, on a compost heap. They break down naturally into compost that enriches garden soil.

4. Reuse and recycle paper and cardboard, or shred them for your compost heap. Make sure the compost heap is properly contained, so it does not attract rats.

5. Ensure trash for collection is sealed to keep out rats and other pests. A rat can gnaw into a plastic garbage bag in less than a second!

Further information

Books

Training Your Pet Rat by Gerry Buscis and Barbara Somerville (Barron's Educational Series, 2000) Encourage your pet's behavior so that it stays healthy and happy.

Oh, Rats! The Story of Rats and People by Albert Marrin (Dutton Books, 2006) The many ways that the lives of rats and people come together.

Web sites

FactHound offers a safe, fun way to find Internet sites related to this book. All of the sites on FactHound have been researched by our staff.
Visit *www.facthound.com* for age-appropriate sites. You may browse subjects by clicking on letters, or by clicking on pictures and words.
FactHound will fetch the best sites for you!

Film

Ratatouille (Disney Pixar, 2007)
Animated film about Remy the rat, who loves food and cooking. He dreams of becoming a chef in Paris and eventually gets his chance in one of the city's finest restaurants.

KEEPING PET RATS

1. Domestic rats make great pets. Like any pet, they need proper care, a suitable enclosure, bedding, and fresh food and water every day.

2. Get advice and read about pet rats before they arrive. Check with people in your house that they are happy about you having pet rats. Who will pay for the rats, supplies, and food?

3. Get your rats from someone who has plenty of experience keeping them. Choose rats that are healthy and strong.

4. Rats are social animals and are best kept in pairs, but of the same sex. Otherwise fights break out and you may soon be overrun with rat youngsters!

5. Properly cared for and handled, pet rats do not bite. But be aware of the small risks. A few people are allergic to rats.

6. Are you prepared to look after your rats, not just now, but for their whole lives—which could be several years? Also, think about who will look after them when you are away.

Index